DAILY REFLECTIONS
WITH JESUS

"Come to Me, all you who labor and are burdened, and I will give you rest" (Matthew 11:25).

DAILY REFLECTIONS WITH JESUS

THIRTY-ONE INSPIRING REFLECTIONS
AND CONCLUDING PRAYERS
PLUS POPULAR PRAYERS TO JESUS

By
REV. RAWLEY MYERS

Illustrated

CATHOLIC BOOK PUBLISHING CORP.
New Jersey

NIHIL OBSTAT: Francis J. McAree, S.T.D.
Censor Librorum

IMPRIMATUR: ✚ Patrick J. Sheridan, D.D.
Vicar General, Archdiocese of New York

(T-740)

PREFACE

A Note about Jesus

THERE is no better way to follow Christ than by talking to Him and visiting with Him, which is prayer, and reflecting upon Him and what He said. Our Faith is not something—it is Someone, the Savior. We must think about Him. And the more we know Him, the more we love Him and want to follow Him. This is what our religion is all about.

You can gain heaven without knowing the names of the vestments the priest wears at Mass or how many candles to light for Benediction or the size of the Vatican, but can you be a Christian and gain eternal life without knowing Christ?

Don't get bogged down in side issues, unimportant matters, trivia. Too many in the Church today play the game of trivial pursuit in religion. What matters is Christ. And He matters most; to know Him, to love Him, to follow Him. And the more you know Jesus the more you will be thrilled about the Faith.

The more you visit Him and reflect upon Him, the more your faith will come alive. Not some dull, if not boring, routine. You will be like the people in Palestine long ago when He came into their village. You will see Him, His face aglow and full of love, and you will listen to Him and say, "No man has ever spoken like this Man."

Jesus is joy, He is love, He is glory. And right now at this very moment He holds out His arms to embrace you.

A Note about You

No one can know Jesus for you. You can only know Him for yourself. I may know a prominent person. I can tell you about him, but this is secondhand knowledge. You will never really know him unless you meet him in person.

The best another individual can do is introduce you to Christ. And then you will get to know Him by visiting Him on your own. I urge you then with all my heart to take time to reflect on Jesus.

When people mature and get over the juvenile notion that life is for fun, they begin, at last, to think seriously and see that Jesus is important. And He alone can make us happy. The trouble is the media night and day inundates us with their phony philosophy that life is to have fun, every day a picnic, "happy time." They do this, of course, to sell their products.

To overcome all such false propaganda is not easy, and some people just never grow up. They have juvenile notions all their lives and act like silly teenagers. How sad.

One is mature when he thinks about Jesus.

CONTENTS

Reflections

Prayers to Jesus

St. Thomas the Apostle accepts the Risen Jesus as his Lord and God.

Day 1

Jesus, Our Joy and Our Hope

THE life of Jesus is incredible to a loveless people. He loves us so much that He gave His life for us. He came on earth to save us from being devoured by our own selfishness. But because we are so self-centered it is most difficult for us to comprehend how Jesus could love us so much.

There is so much pride in our day. Few people seem to see things as they are. And so many people are unhappy. Bishop Sheen said, "Never in the history of the world have so many people been so unhappy as they are today." They are unhappy because they think they can buy happiness. But it is not for sale.

Jesus is our model. He alone can show us the way to be happy in this world and to gain eternal happiness in the life to come. Christ is the source of all joy and of everlasting enthusiasm.

The Risen Christ, marked with the five wounds, is our hope. He in glory prays before the Father, and when we pray we pray with Him, and the Father embraces Him and embraces us. What could be more wonderful on this earth?

Christ is certitude. He is music, song, and sunshine. With Jesus there is no room for gloom, no room for mediocrity. Jesus is joy, if one truly knows Him. We come to know Him through prayer, for prayer is visiting with our Lord. Christ alone reveals the true meaning of our humanity.

Prayer

O JESUS, even when You were weary of limb, You had time for sinners. Come to my assistance. Bless me, help me. Your love is ever searching for souls. You pursue us constantly.

Give me the grace and the courage to turn to You in prayer so You can give Your gracious graces to me and my loved ones. Amen.

The Archangel Gabriel tells Mary that her Son will be the Son of God and Savior.

Day 2

Jesus, Son of the Living God

WHY, unless God loves us, should He have given us His only Son? The Incarnation was a torrential invasion of God's love, so great that it overwhelms us.

Here on earth Christ founded a kingdom of love. In the Our Father we pray that it will prosper. But it is opposed by so many forces in our society. We must pray all the more that love will overcome hostility, that the kingdom of Christ will be victorious over the Evil One. Proud, power-hungry men in His day would not listen to Christ. Then, as now, they did not want Him around.

We must give Jesus a chance in our lives so that we may become Christlike. He gave the example for us so that we may do as He did. He is our model. Our goal is to imitate Christ.

One night long ago the cry of a Child was heard in a manger, and ever since the world has not been able to silence that cry. People everywhere have tried to do so. In our day they do not directly oppose Jesus—they just ridicule religion. They call it old fashioned and out of date.

The enemies of Christ sway the crowd by telling them what they want to hear. And they make money on having our society think childishly that life is all playtime. They promote this notion in every way through the media, and then "laugh all the way to the bank" at the stupidity of the public. And Jesus weeps.

Prayer

DEAR Jesus, the Incarnation is God bowing down to us. You came to be with us to help us. Thank You, Lord. This tremendous event showed once and for all Your great and overwhelming love for us. Thank You, Jesus.

But bless me, O Christ, so that I will take advantage of Your love and turn to You and pray to You and grow in soul. Amen.

After preaching in His hometown,
Jesus is rejected by His own people.

Day 3

Jesus, Rejected by the World

"HE came unto His own and His own received Him not." He was, from a worldly point of view, a failure. He lived in Palestine, a place of no importance. No one took seriously this little land. He was born in a cave, not a palace. When God became Man He chose a poor woman, quiet and gentle, for His Mother. He as a teacher selected fishermen for His companions and He preached to the poor.

He did not even try to impress the important people. In fact, He had the unfortunate habit of telling the truth to the Pharisees, that they were hypocrites. When one is perfectly honest with proud people you can be sure that person will have to pay for it. But God has a way of snatching victory from defeat. And so it was with Jesus. Easter followed Good Friday.

When He preached, Jesus proposed poverty as a clearer way to see God; money gets in the way.

Jesus taught that life is a struggle, but this purifies the soul and makes us better people.

God sent His Son Who was abject and despised. God does not most often reveal Himself in glory. He hides in humble hearts, in the poor in spirit, whom Jesus called blessed. His followers are humble and hidden. We know from our own experience that the Holy Spirit seldom floods our minds and hearts with great light and courage, as we would like, but rather invites us along quietly amid many ambiguities.

"Be like a child," Jesus said, "and you will enter the heavenly kingdom."

Prayer

O JESUS, Your Saints lived, despite many different circumstances, with great faith in You. They had numerous trials and temptations, but they never gave up trusting You.

Help me to have faith like theirs. Help me to believe in You always, and, like Your holy Mother, be loyal and true to You to the end. Amen.

Jesus chooses twelve ordinary men to be
His followers and bear witness to Him.

Day 4

Jesus, Our Model

JESUS chose a motley group to be His
Apostles. They were unpredictable, unreli-
able, and, at the end, unfaithful. He gave them
graces and changed them, as He will also
change us if we let Him. And after Pentecost
they became great teachers and martyrs for
Christ. There is hope for the hopeless.

We must follow Christ. To serve is to image
Jesus. Why did He walk the roads of
Palestine? Why did He live with the poor and
outcasts and search out sinners? Why did He
let His enemies arrest Him and beat Him and
curse Him and kill Him? Because He loves
us. Because He dearly cares for us, because

16

He wanted to save us from the hellish sea of selfishness in which mankind was drowning.

We are to be Christlike, to be the compassionate Christ. We do not walk alone. He is always with us. The whole world needs Christ. We have Him. We must give Him to those who are groping blindly in the darkness. We are to take Him to the starving in soul.

John the Baptist, the prophet, declared that the great Person was coming. "He must increase, I must decrease." He warned the people, telling them to repent: "Save yourself from the wrath to come." When Jesus came to the Jordan John announced that this was the Holy One of God.

Jesus showed this in what He said and did. He spoke with the wisdom of heaven. He said the most beautiful things ever uttered on the earth. He healed with many miracles. He was the Savior.

Prayer

JESUS, You Who sweat blood and gave Your life for me—can You be deaf to my cries for mercy? Even when tortured and heartsick on the Cross, Your thoughts were mostly of others and helping them.

Please help me. I am in need. I am weak and sick of soul. Without Your blessings I will perish. Without Your grace I can do nothing. Please help me. Amen.

The sick are brought to Jesus, and He heals many of their afflictions.

Day 5

Jesus, Our Healer

BE like Jesus and pray to God trustingly. Be like a child in faith, and, by your love and kindness and courtesy strengthen the love of others. Jesus said of His followers, "By their fruits you will know them." Live lovingly. Ease and self-satisfaction are for the worldy-minded. Jesus did not take this road.

Christ did not have an attitude of gloom toward life or toward death. He was sad because many would not listen to His message, but He delighted in nature and He delighted in people who were interested in God. He was stern with the mean-hearted and unloving, but He was also very kind to those who suffered

18

and were troubled. Ever friendly and considerate, Jesus told us in the Beatitudes how we can be happy.

His joy was deep and abiding. He wanted to share this with us. To be fulfilled we must strive to be our best. Realize your potentialities and you will know a deep satisfaction. Never be satisfied with doing nothing.

He taught that men are not animals or Angels. Humans are body and soul, "living souls inbreathed by God."

John Keats, the great poet, spoke of this world as "a vale of soul-making." This is what Jesus taught. Here we are purified to prepare for paradise in the next life. As one spiritual writer put it, "In Jesus' teaching life is a trust committed to everyone. We will have to give an account of this trust. It is what a person makes of his gifts, stage by stage in life, that makes him to be what he is. Will the Son of Man be ashamed of him or say, 'Well done, good and faithful servant'?"

Prayer

JESUS, in our day, many do not think about You but then worry themselves to death. You are the answer. Help people to see this.

Many think they have no time to pray. What fools! They are ever nervous and restless because they do not listen to You. Please open up their ears. Amen.

*Jesus preaches the Sermon on the Mount,
teaching the people the heart of His message.*

Day 6

Jesus, Eternal Wisdom

THE words of Jesus provide food for thought beyond anything or anyone else in the world. They are a permanent addition to the wisdom of the world.

Jesus in the Temple praised the poor widow for giving her penny to the needy. Far greater was her gift, taken from her food money, than the contributions of the rich who with show gave what was leftover.

Jesus told us to spread His message. "Shout it from the housetops," He said. You put a candle on a candlestick to give light to the room. "In the same way your light must shine before men so that many know the good news and praise God."

He said, "Do not lay up riches on earth." Store up heavenly treasures. Where your treasure is, there is your heart.

Jesus said, "Whoever would save his life will lose it; whoever loses his life will save it. What does it profit a man to gain the whole world and lose his own immortal soul? If anyone is ashamed of Me on earth, I will be ashamed of him in heaven."

Our lives, Jesus shows us, are not nothing. They have meaning and purpose. We celebrate a future with Him. Every Eucharistic celebration, the Mass, reminds us of this.

We come unknowing and without invitation into the world, but if in our searching we find Christ we have found riches.

Prayer

O JESUS, when we look at the night sky we see the majesty of God; when we look at the purple mountains we see His greatness; when we look at the sea, as far as the eye can see, we realize His might and power.

We listen to the songbird and know His love; we look at the vistas and valleys, at sunny days and green fields and know His joy. Praise God. Amen.

Jesus says that God will take care of us, just as
He cares for the lilies of the field.

Day 7

Jesus, Our Refuge

JESUS is a Person Who made numerous claims, gave many striking pieces of advice, spoke a number of strange rebukes, and told a series of strangely beautiful stories. He came for everyone. Like the sun He shines for all.

Jesus told us not to worry, any more than the birds do. God takes care of them and He takes care of us. Why then are we so anxious? Trust Him.

If a person never heard of the Gospel and read it for the first time, he would say that truly this is an individual Who is different. The people said this in His day: "No man ever spoke like this Man." There is in Him some-thing that is mysterious and many-sided.

Jesus made tremendous claims. He is either a Divine Person or a fraud and a liar. He said, "Before Abraham was, I am."

In the Gospel we find Jesus is the most merciful judge and the kindest and most sympathetic friend. He is unique in history. There is no other person like Him. He told us He came from heaven to guide us back to heaven. This surely is the thing we want most of all. If we follow Him we are on the road to happiness in this life and in the next.

Jesus said the most beautiful things ever uttered by any human. He is original. He star-tled the people by saying such things as, "In My kingdom the last shall be first." He called us to be humble, whereas all the leaders of the world were pompous and had everyone bowing before them. But Jesus was so differ-ent. He does not look at bankbooks or scrap-books; He looks into the heart.

Prayer

JESUS, You say, "Stay with Me and I will stay with you." The vine must be united to the branch or it shrivels up and dies and is worthless. I am nothing without You.

Do not let me be proud and spoil every-thing I try to do for You. Be with me. Bless me. Make me humble. Amen.

Jesus calls for love of neighbor: "Treat others as you would have them treat you."

Day 8

Jesus, Full of Goodness and Love

THE wisdom of the world is not the wisdom of Christ. In fact, most often, it is just the opposite. Christ told us we would find happiness in being unselfish. The world tells us to be selfish, seek money for oneself, pleasure, power, popularity.

His is the love that teaches us how to love. True love is in giving, not receiving. We are so mixed up these days that many think love is simply sex. Or if not that simplistic, at least that love is how another can make me happy.

But we are to imitate Christ, and He was a most giving Person. The Creator is holy Love. Jesus was a Man of love. He was a self-offer-

24

ing Person. The Father was all in all to Jesus. He no more thought of Himself and His goodness than a rose thinks of its breathless beauty. And because He loved the Father He loved His children.

This is what we are supposed to do as well. Jesus never asks the impossible. We can do this with His help. We should change our way of thinking, not asking what others can do for us, but what we can do for others.

Jesus helps us. He gained all the graces we need; His grace unites us to Himself. He dwells within us and vivifies our actions. Christ is our refuge; He protects our soul. But more, He blesses us so that we can be less self-thinking and more thoughtful of others.

Jesus came to earth and made holy what in the beginning God had already declared to be good. But then selfishness took over. Man became proud and pride ruins everything. Man tried to run the world on his own and he went from disaster to disaster. But God rescued us. He sent Jesus.

Prayer

DEAR Jesus, You tirelessly seek souls. We are so weak and so blind that we do not pray to You as we should. Please help us.

Let me not be so foolish as to forget You. I need You, Jesus. I need Your grace. With all my heart I beg Your blessings. Amen.

Because of the faith of a crippled man, Jesus for-gives his sins and cures him.

Day 9

Jesus, Patient and Most Merciful

JESUS was a teacher of wisdom. How little wisdom there is in the world today. You would think everyone would look to Christ and listen to Him. We need wisdom so badly. But often it is just the opposite. Because we are proud, because advertising flatters us so much and we gullibly believe it, we listen to no one. And we go deeper every day into the swamp.

Jesus was a healer of bodies, but most of all a healer of souls. He was a mediator of the sacred. He began His mission by saying, "The Spirit of the Lord is upon Me."

He was filled with compassion. For Jesus, compassion was the great quality of God. He said, "Be compassionate as God is compassionate." Compassion means "to feel with," being moved by suffering. It is mercy and being merciful. Mercy is the heart and core of Jesus.

Jesus was so humble, but He was also strong in upholding the truth. Hence He was frequently in conflict with the proud who were forever critical of His every word and deed. He would not back down when the truth was involved.

Wisdom is central to the teachings of Jesus. He was a channel of Divine Wisdom. He brought the wisdom of God to earth. There is a wise way to take on our journey and a foolish way. Jesus shows us the wise way.

Prayer

ON the Cross, dear Jesus, Your face was covered with blood, Your lips and throat were parched and suffering. Yet You refused the wine. It was the only time You asked for something for Yourself, and yet You refused even this comfort. You wanted us to know You thirsted for souls. Your great desire always was for souls.

Enable us to help You. You endured the intolerable suffering on the Cross to gain the graces we need. Help us, Lord. Amen.

Afraid for their lives, the disciples have recourse to Jesus and He calms a storm.

Day 10

Jesus, Lover of Prayer

OUR hearts are faint and we fret and worry, but Jesus looks after us. Our lives are in His care. Jesus ever waits and watches at our hearts to come in and bring us His love. Until He enters, the house is empty. But then He comes, and fear is cast out by His love.

Man who is made in the image of God must know Him or be desolate. We are here to praise God as Christ did. When life is a mere yielding to passions, all is disorder. When an individual, made for God, clings to the false pleasures of the world, he is unhappy.

It is prayer that helps us the most. In prayer we visit with Jesus. So many in this world are in the dungeon of despair, moping about in self-pity. We must help them to know Christ. Jesus was forever helping others. His arms are always stretched out to receive souls.

All our talk and many words contribute little to making a better world. Prayer contributes greatly. We must pray for faith so we will not be lost travelers in the world. It is prayer that brings the blessings of God. We are not self-sufficient. We badly, badly need His holy assistance.

Do not let the spiritual be crowded out of your life. Prayer can turn things around. In prayer we become what Jesus wants us to be. In prayer we rest in His arms. We are unhappy when we are self-centered. We are happy when Christ embraces us and we walk with Jesus in joy.

Prayer

BE with me, my Savior, all the day long. Be at my side, dear Jesus, and I will not fear. Walk with me, Jesus, and let me walk with You and I will be more like You.

Hold my hand, O Lord, I am like a man on a stormy, choppy sea. I reach out to You, dear Jesus. I know You will save me. Give me Your grace so that I can find safety and warmth in Your dear, dear arms. Amen.

Jesus says the Bread that He will give is His Flesh for the life of the world.

Day 11

Jesus, Bread of Heaven

"**I** AM the Bread that came down from heaven," Jesus said. "He who eats of this Bread will live forever."

Murmurs broke out at this. "Impossible," many people said. "Who can hear such a thing?" And so some left Him. Jesus turned to the Apostles and said, "Will you also go away?" Peter answered, "Lord, to whom shall we go? We know and believe that You have the words of eternal life. You are the Christ, the Son of God."

Another time Jesus said, "If you listen to Me, you shall know the truth." He said, "Abraham rejoiced to see My day: he saw it and was glad." Some said in surprise, "You are not yet fifty; have you seen Abraham?" Jesus replied, "Before Abraham came to be—I am."

His brilliant words astounded them.

Turn to Jesus in every trouble; with faith follow Him. Offer Him your love and loyalty; ask Him to enrich you with His grace.

Jesus loved sinners and mingled with them; His mission was saving them and infusing new love into them and changing their anger into love.

Jesus promised love to all who go to Him. He helps us. He is the Lamb, the Peacemaker between God and man. He preached especially to the common people. This, of course, flies in the face of our notion that money makes a person important. Jesus' kindness surpasses by far the kindness of the most loving mother, which is the most beautiful love in the world.

Prayer

GIVE us silence, dear Jesus, so that we can pray and praise You. Lead us aside from the noise and busyness of our world. Then we can be with You and listen to You and love You.

Heal us in body and soul. Have mercy on us, dear Lord, and on all who are in need, especially our relatives and friends and neighbors. Be our light and strength. Amen.

During His Public Ministry, Jesus tells the Apostles about His coming Death and Resurrection.

Day 12

Jesus, Father of the Poor

JESUS was not impressed by the rich and famous. He had no desire for wealth and luxury. Rather, as He said, these more often ruin a person than help him. He Himself "had nowhere to lay His head." Living His life in poverty, He showed that money is not the greatest thing in life, as many moderns feel. They are ignorant. We often see that the lives of poor families are more happy than the rich, for the wealthy are always anxious about their money.

Jesus was always honest. At times this made Him feel like a stranger in the world. So many are devious. And because He would not flatter the proud and the powerful, He was put to death. For He told them point blank that they were hypocrites. He said they were "whited sepulchers;" they were like tombs chiseled out of rocks. Whitewashed on the outside they looked very nice; inside they were full of dead men's bones.

Jesus came from heaven to speak the truth to humans. And He continued to tell the truth even when it cost Him His life. Christ's words were as straight and as swift as a thunderbolt. They struck the heart and made men think.

He did not avoid the storm when it came to telling the truth. He did not hesitate to say, "The Father and I are one." He was a Divine Person and He spoke not with earthly wisdom but with heavenly wisdom. The truth was uppermost in His mind, even though it led to His crucifixion.

Prayer

O JESUS, many have gone astray. Who will feed them? They are wandering away from You. Please help them. Bring them back. Give us hearts and love to help You. Send us apostolic souls to labor for You.

Dear Jesus, let us enter the field ripe for the harvest. Too many who call themselves Your followers stand on the sideline. But that is not being a Christ-follower. Send us many who are true to You. Amen.

Jesus tells the Apostles to let the little children come to Him and then blesses the children.

Day 13

Jesus, Lover of Children

ONE cannot explain Jesus. A person cannot express the inexpressible. The warmth of His embrace, the pleasure of His company, the joy of being with Him cannot be expressed in words. To talk of Christ is like trying to capture in words the colors of the rainbow.

Jesus said, "A good tree bears good fruit; a bad tree, bad fruit. Judge a tree by the fruit that it bears." He said, "Anyone who hears My words but does not practice them is building his house upon sandy ground."

Jesus took a little child and stood him in the midst of them and putting His arms

34

around him said, "If anyone wishes to be the greatest he must be like this child."

Jesus said, "Do not judge another or you will be judged in the same way." He said, "Treat others the way you would have them treat you."

People brought their children to Jesus. The Apostles said He was too tired and they should go away. But Jesus said, "Let the little children come to Me, for of such is the kingdom of Heaven." And He then embraced the little ones and, placing His hands on them, blessed them.

They came to Jericho. A blind beggar hearing it was Jesus, called out, "Jesus, have pity on me." Some scolded him and told him to be quiet. But he shouted out all the louder. Jesus stopped. "What do you wish?", He asked. "Lord, that I may see." Jesus said, "Be healed. Your faith has cured you."

Prayer

LORD, do not let me seek what is false and do what is futile. What a petty, spoiled, and childish person I am. I trust You, Jesus. You hear when I call.

Come to my assistance. Lift me to the light and put joy into my heart. Thanksgiving, glory, and praise to You Whose love is enduring. Keep me in Your love forever. Amen.

Jesus has compassion on a leper and takes away his disease, giving him peace.

Day 14

Jesus, Our Peace and Reconciliation

WITH St. Paul we should say, "It is no longer I who live, but Christ Who lives in me." I put on Christ. I think with the mind of Christ, I love with the heart of Christ. Christ tells us to love. Make love paramount in our hearts. Hell is not to love anymore.

We are the people for whom Christ was crucified. We must beg His forgiveness, beg His assistance. Christian living is being faithful to Christ. St. Paul said, "None of us lives to himself. If we live, we live to the Lord, and if we die, we die to the Lord. So then, whether we live or whether we die, we are the Lord's."

We are set free by Christ, no longer slaves to sin and death. Whom do you belong to, whom are you living for? St. Paul said, "I have been crucified with Christ . . . and the life I now live . . . I live by faith in the Son of God, Who loved me and gave Himself for me."

Amid trials and tribulations we look to Christ. We need His daily blessings or we will perish. Jesus is not distant, cold, and unapproachable. He is here, gracious and merciful, abounding in love. Jesus, "God with us," is full of mercy. The Psalmist says of God, "As a father has compassion for his children, so the Lord has compassion on those who seek Him."

In Jesus, God entered history and was a suffering God, a God Who wore our weakness, felt our fear and loneliness.

Jesus said, "I come not to be served but to serve." He was a suffering servant. He said, "I give My life as a ransom for many."

Prayer

JESUS, bless us. St. Gregory said of You, "Christ has led us out of captivity because He has swallowed up our corruption in the power of His incorruption."

You are especially with sinners, the outcasts, poor, and despised. We are most grateful. Even in Your agony on the Cross love continued to flow from Your Sacred Heart. Thank You. Amen.

In His infinite goodness, Jesus cures a deaf mute.

Day 15

Jesus, Infinite Goodness

THE Lord is our joy. He Who loved was assassinated by hate. Christ taught us it is better to go down to defeat in the eyes of the world than to win a false victory of popularity.

His friendship for us expresses itself in silence. It is in silence that we meet Him and come to know His great love. It is difficult to find a place of silence in our noisy and busy world. Is this why few seem to know Him?

In silence Jesus speaks our name and we answer, as Mary did, "Master."

He was so generous. After a long day of apostolic work, the crowds came to Him again. After sunset they brought Him their sick, and Jesus, ever kind, healed them. To Him the sick are sacred. That night, there were many hearts with newborn joy who had been healed by Jesus, unchained from their pain and suffering. Many households rejoiced; their loved one who had been sick was cured.

Christ was a friend to all. And He was a perpetual surprise. His goodness was so great that people could hardly believe it. We must look to Him.

Today the machine of life is moving faster and faster; the merry-go-round is spinning more quickly. We must stop and take time to think or we will be lost. There is great inertia in the hearts of many. Their souls are asleep. Humans compared to Christ are only half alive. Christ challenges us. From Christ comes new life.

Prayer

JESUS, I pray for the elderly, the homeless, for family and friends. Please assist the sick. Be with those, Lord, who are dying today. Turn hardened hearts to kindness. Amid all the uncertainties of life, give us confidence.

Have mercy on all who are in need. Have pity on them; have pity on us. See our tears and hold our hands. Amen.

At the Transfiguration, Jesus appears to the Apostles in all His Divine splendor.

Day 16

Jesus, Splendor of the Father

JESUS spoke of the Father as One Who makes the sun to shine upon all. His gifts are for all; they are the lavish blessings of His great heart, an overflowing effulgence of His great goodness. When, in a parable someone complained, Jesus had God say, "Do you begrudge My generosity?"

This theme of the goodness of God runs through the Parable of the Prodigal Son, which should be called the Generous Father. The father is so wonderful to the wayward boy it is almost impossible to believe. No human father would be so generous. But, in this story, the Father is God.

Jesus in His teachings subverted the earth-bound thinking of the world. What is the way that leads to eternal life? It is Christ-centered living, a deepening relationship and friendship with Christ. And a gracious God is at the core of the teachings of Jesus.

Jesus said, "I stand at the door knocking." Jesus, with His love and His many gifts, wishes to enter, and when we let Him our hearts are filled with light and goodness. When one's heart is centered on Christ then death is not to be feared or a cause for despair as with pagans. It is the transforming point when we pass from life here to life hereafter. And suffering is not a curse but something that purifies the soul so we can be more Christlike.

Jesus preached the road less traveled. Secular wisdom says seek wealth, popularity, pleasure, power; Jesus says seek humility. We cannot find true satisfaction in this life.

Prayer

O JESUS, holy are Your ways, holy the journey of life with You. Holy is the way from captivity to freedom. Holy is the joy You give us, holy the trials we endure.

Holy are homes and families when You are in our homes. Holy are teachers and friends. Holy is death when You are at our side. And holy is our homecoming to embrace You in heaven. Amen.

*Jesus tells the people that they are to hear the
Word of God and keep it.*

Day 17

Jesus, Zealous for Souls

THE people were amazed at the teachings
of Jesus. He taught with authority, unlike
the other rabbis. He spoke in a fresh and
striking way. He clearly pointed out what
God demanded of His people. He was masterful and vivid. His message, the people felt,
came straight from God. And so it did.

He gave forth the impression of strength,
confidence, and the conviction that He was
speaking on God's behalf. He never doubted
this. He was God's representative, the fore-
told Messiah. This sense of Jesus was overwhelming. Jesus set out to "seek and save"
souls. He cared deeply for people. He was

happy in the company of the poor and simple; He loved children.

Jesus only spoke sternly when He was outraged by the meanness, arrogance, cruelty, and hostility of the proud. They hated Him because they were jealous. He was taking the people away from them.

Jesus told the people to live as befits children of God. The kingdom is for the generous. Jesus said the Father was loving to all His children. He did not think of God as sentimental and easygoing, one of the fallacies of our day. A good father, after all, must sometimes punish a wayward child for his own good, even if the child cannot understand this, as we cannot understand our trials and suffering. Jesus told us that we should show our love for the Father by helping His children, our neighbors.

Prayer

DEAREST Jesus, at the foot of the Cross Your dear Mother, though brokenhearted and in tears, bowed her head, and, hard as it was, accepted the Will of God.

Help us to bow to the sorrow that comes to us in life, and, with the Blessed Mother offer it up to God. Let us too pray for Your help because we know we cannot suffer alone. Amen.

Jesus tells Martha and Mary that prayerful union with Him is more important than all else.

Day 18

Jesus, Our Way and Our Life

THE life of Jesus cannot be written. It must be learned in prayer. Jesus said, "Learn of Me." We learn of Him when we pray faithfully.

Jesus flashed like a meteor across the sky, and He has influenced mankind ever since. His sheer influence on people's thought in every age and His incomparable contribution to goodness on earth is beyond description.

There is a great emotion experienced in speaking of Him, for Him, and against Him. His true followers follow Jesus, Man of compassion, with deep devotion. He is admired for His sacrifice, surrender, and suffering for us. He is no stranger to those who pray. However, His personality and charism are baffling to those who do not pray.

To know Christ is a thrilling experience, this Person Whose life is the most tremendous drama in human history, Whose apparent failure was His overwhelming success. The death of Jesus bitterly disappointed all the disciples' high hopes. But then on Easter everything was reversed and joy followed sorrow, and His continued presence with us is our glory.

Jesus is the way to God. United to Him as the vine to the branch, our strength is His strength. Christ is, as St. Paul said, "the supreme manifestation of the love of God."

He, our Savior, suffered to save us. He was arrested while praying. Judas led the temple guards to Him. Pretending to embrace Jesus, Judas betrayed Him with a kiss. The guards seized Jesus. All the Apostles "fled into the night."

Prayer

O JESUS, we thank You for coming to us, for rescuing us from the powers of darkness and bringing us into the kingdom of love. May Your peace reign in our hearts. May we grow in love and hope and faith.

Give us salvation, O Savior. Fulfill our needs according to Your great generosity. To You be glory forever. Amen.

Jesus forgives a penitent woman's sins and allows her to wash His feet with her tears.

Day 19

Jesus, Friend of the Outcast

THE wisdom of this world is foolish, the fads and fashions of the crowds are senseless; so many are self-centered and thoughtless. They do not live a life, they only follow the others. But Jesus taught, "You cannot serve two masters." We must choose. We can follow the silly crowd going nowhere, or we can follow Jesus on the royal road to heaven.

Jesus said, "You cannot get grapes from a bramble bush." "If a blind person leads a blind person, they both fall into the ditch." "You strain at the gnat and swallow the camel."

Life in this world is often grim. Christ is our hope. In our days of anxious striving, He will comfort us. We are afraid many times not to conform to the fashion of the day. But Jesus spoke out strongly against blind conformity.

He Himself ate with outcasts. He was not seen with the right people. He decried the pomposity and false solutions given off in the name of scholarship. He knew that in truth even the greatest human thinkers were small in mind. He asked us not to be small in heart as well.

Jesus ridiculed those who were concerned with honors. He castigated the crowd-pleasers, and indicted the self-opinionated. The proud saw all this as offensive, threatening and dangerous. They heard Him but did not listen. Let us pray that we are not like them. Jesus invites us to see reality, the flowers, the birds, as gifts of a generous and gracious Father.

Prayer

GIVE us, dear Lord, more Christlike hearts so that we will reach out and touch others with Your love. Help us to bring the message of Your goodness to the confused world. There is already too much anger and hostility.

Give Your people peace of heart. Those who spread Your love are the ones most loved by You. Dear Jesus, help us do more kind deeds. Amen.

Jesus enters Jerusalem in triumph, with the people acclaiming Him as the Messiah.

Day 20

Jesus, the Man for Others

THE proud did not listen to Jesus when He was on earth, and they do not listen to Him today. He boldly refuted them but He was under no illusions. He knew that though they could not answer Him, they would destroy Him. This is the way pride works, then and now.

Though He knew He would be put to death, He bravely went up to Jerusalem to face His fate, to do the Father's Will. He entered the great city as the people formed a parade to welcome Him, waving palm branches. And in Jerusalem, despite the plots going on all around, He, a masterful figure continued to teach the people. He would not bow to fear.

Jesus told them they must be children to enter the kingdom of heaven. Childlike, they must have simplicity of faith, trust, and goodness of heart. He was speaking not only to them but to us. So many now do not have a simple, childlike faith; they think they are sophisticated and knowledgeable and believe little. They are cynical and skeptical and trust no one, not even God.

But Jesus insisted that a person's place in God's kingdom would be determined by his willingness to love openly as children do and to serve others. Every follower must be like Jesus Himself, "a Man for others."

Jesus drove the merchants from the temple. "My house is a house of prayer and you have made it a den of thieves," He said. Will you drive the materialistic distractions from your soul and make it a house of prayer?

Prayer

O CHRIST, do not let me be lulled into complacency by TV. It puts minds to sleep. Let me rather look at You on the Cross and think about all You did for me. Help me to beg Your forgiveness and ask Your blessings and graces.

Your death on the Cross changed the world. Let reflection on the crucifix change my life and make it not self-centered but Christ-centered. Thank You. Amen.

*Jesus performs the miracle of the loaves, which is
a sign of the Eucharist.*

Day 21

Jesus, the Hidden Manna

JESUS laid down His life as a testimony of
His love for us. And the night before His
death, He gave us, out of love, love unutter-
able, the Blessed Eucharist, a most lavish
gift. It was the perfect way of expressing His
love. It is only because the Body of Jesus was
broken and mangled on the Cross that it
could become our spiritual food at the Last
Supper. And at every Communion table ever
since, the disciples of Christ are gathering
the fruits of Calvary. We receive Jesus Who
was sacrificed for us and we obtain the
graces that He gained by that sacrifice.

The Eucharist is His greatest gift to men.
At the Last Supper, the Apostles were filled

with a vague foreboding of impending disaster. All eyes were fixed on Him Whose words had signified all too clearly that a crisis was coming.

He said, "With desire I have desired to eat this passover meal with you, before I suffer." He was about to perform the great act that would forever perpetuate His presence among men. He took the bread and said, "This is My Body." He gave it to them. No word broke the great silence. He took the chalice and said solemnly, "This is My Blood," and gave it to them. "Do this in memory of Me," He said. And the Apostles, full of wonder, received the Eucharist.

By this act Jesus devised a superhuman means to stay on earth among men whom He loved with all His heart. In the Eucharist, Jesus placed Himself at the mercy of men. But Divine Love is so intense that it does not calculate disadvantages; it only plunges on headlong, risking indifference and irreverence to gain the hearts of a few.

Prayer

BE ever with us, O Christ. Our hearts are often cowardly; give us courage. We are often confused; give us light.

We are fearful of the past and of the future. Be with us. Assist us in doing Your work and in spreading Your love. Amen.

*At the Last Supper, Jesus institutes the Holy
Sacrifice of the Mass.*

Day 22

Jesus, God's Greatest Gift

JESUS gave us the Mass, our greatest prayer. For at Mass we pray with Christ. At Mass, with Christ, we experience a profound oneness with Him in this glorious act of praise. Here one falls in love with Christ.

St. Thomas Aquinas wrote of the Eucharist:

Godhead here in hiding, Whom I adore,
Masked by these bare shadows, shape,
and nothing more,
See, Lord, at Thy service low lies here a
heart,
Lost, all lost in wonder, at the God Thou
art.

We do nothing in this world that is more important than going to Mass and being with Jesus and praying with Him.

At Mass, we pour out our hearts: God of our childhood, bless our parents who did everything for us. God of our youth, You saw us through turbulent times; bless our teachers and our friends. God of our maturity, You showed us about life and love. God of our old age, You taught us to pray. As our bodies decrease in strength, give strength to our souls.

At Mass, Christ gives us His choicest blessings. The Heart of Jesus is full of limitless love. When we open our hearts to Him, Jesus yields a torrent of graces.

Prayer

JESUS, You were taken prisoner to set us free. You were crowned with thorns to make us kings. We are grateful.

Have mercy on me, Jesus. You died on the Cross to give me life. Help me to serve You. Amen.

After a huge catch of fish, Jesus tells St. Peter that henceforth he "shall catch men."

Day 23

Jesus, Founder of the Church

JESUS gave us the Church to guide us in life. When He returned to the Father, He did not want to leave us alone. He gave us the Church to teach as He taught, to carry on His work in the world.

We meet Christ in His Church. Jesus said to the Church, "He who hears you, hears Me." The Church through the ages has been an extension of the Incarnation. She has a tenderness in forgiving, as Jesus did. She has from Jesus the power to sanctify souls, to impart graces acquired by Christ suffering on the Cross. In the Church we are united to Christ.

Since our life-goal is to be Christlike, no one can help us more in this than His Church. The Church is the custodian of the truth He brought from heaven. She teaches her children to live in the Image of Christ, to pray for the guidance of the Holy Spirit, to love with the love of the Sacred Heart.

That the Church has a human side is evident. Men of authority fail and make mistakes. However such things may be, Christ promised that the Church would never fail us as our guide to heaven.

He said, "You are Peter [the rock] and upon this rock I will build My Church and the gates of hell shall not prevail against it." The forces of evil will never triumph over the Church insofar as it is the guide leading us to eternal life. We need this guide. Humans are so very vulnerable to every passing fad.

Prayer

JESUS, protect Your Church. Help it, bless it, and direct it in these most troubled times. The true history of the Church is about Saints, holy men and women in every age who, following the Church, gained heaven.

May the Church always show us the Saints. They teach us how to live the Faith, especially in times of confusion. Thank You for the Church; thank You for the Saints. Amen.

*Jesus tells the Apostles about the joys
and bliss of heaven.*

Day 24

Jesus, Our Teacher

IN this ever-changing world, we cannot find meaning. Material things and worldly values, if we put all our hope in them, lead to darkness and despair. Our hearts yearn for something more. Jesus encourages us to seek the things of heaven, to walk along the path to God with Him. He gives peace to our hearts and trust to our minds. He leads us from the slavery of sin to goodness, from the bondage of self-preoccupation to the freedom of self-forgetfulness.

Jesus was a teacher of great wisdom, for His wisdom is the wisdom of God. Jesus is the Son of the Father, the only-begotten One, Light from Light. And so when John the Baptist saw Him he said, "Behold the Lamb of God."

St. Paul spoke of Jesus as the Wisdom of God, telling us that because of Christ we are made right with God by grace. He said that the wisdom of God is the opposite of the wisdom of this world.

St. Paul stated that he proclaimed Christ crucified, a stumbling block to Jews and foolish to Gentiles. Indeed, he said, "Christ is the Image of the invisible God." St. John related that Christ, the Son of God, "became flesh and dwelt among us."

Jesus gives us a message of great hope in this bleak world. He does not will our present condition but wishes to forgive us and bless us.

Prayer

JESUS, I put my hand in Your hand, as I make my journey to everlasting life. You have laid Your hands upon me, You have called me by name to follow You. Be with me always. Do not let me wander away from You.

You are light in our darkness, comfort for our sadness, bread to nourish us, life that overcomes death. Give us Your grace so that we can sing Your glory and praise God forever. Amen.

Overwhelmed in His Agony by the sins of the world, Jesus is comforted by an Angel.

Day 25

Jesus, Propitiation for Our Sins

JESUS was arrested in the garden and taken to the Temple and into the residence of the high priest next door. The trial that ensued was a mockery. When Jesus remained silent, He was ridiculed. When once He answered, a guard struck Him. The false witnesses lied and contradicted each other. The case was in shambles. To save the situation, the high priest stood up and declared Him guilty.

Jesus was taken to Pontius Pilate, the Roman governor. Pilate knew He was innocent but was too weak to free Him. His soldiers made a crown of thorns and pushed it down on the head of Christ and blood spurted out. And they beat Him and then forced Him to carry the Cross.

On Calvary, Christ showed no sign of fear. They drove huge spikes through His hands and feet. The pain was agonizing. On the Cross, He suffered three hours of terrible torture. He died. A soldier thrust a spear into the side of Jesus to be sure He was dead. The dreadful ordeal was over.

The Apostles were in despair. They had thought Jesus would lead them to victory over sin and darkness. And, on Easter Sunday, He did.

Prayer

JESUS, I pray for my family. Help each one of us. I pray for our home, and for all homes. Bless parents and children.

Especially bless those parents in these difficult days who are trying to raise decent children. It is so hard with all the evil influence all around us. Bless young people having to grow up in an environment where the media features sex and violence. Amen.

Bruised and beaten, Jesus is shown to the crowd by Pilate and then condemned to death.

Day 26

Jesus, Bruised for Our Offenses

WHEN, at the end Jesus stood before Pilate, the governor, unknown to himself, pronounced sentence in the most momentous trial in all of human history. Jesus was innocent as Pilate knew, but was declared guilty. Then Pilate, the weak and petty politician, put on a performance, the silliest thing possible. On the balcony, he washed his hands, he who alone could command Jesus' death, and said that he was innocent of the blood of this just Man. O how humans try to fool themselves, then and now.

What was Christ's crime? Rebellion? Terrorism? No, only helping people and preaching love. But the powerful determined He must die. Evil-minded men cannot stand the good.

Before He was murdered He was tortured and scourged. His body was bruised and bloody all over. And they fixed a crown of thorns and pressed it down on the head of the royal pretender. They did not know His kingdom was not of this world, and so they scoffed at Him for having the mad temerity to claim a kingdom.

Christ was crucified. For anyone who has a heart, crucifixion is a disgusting spectacle. Christ was nailed alive to the wood. The Cross was raised. The mob went into fits of raving madness.

They watched, hoping He would cry out. But He only said softly, "Father, forgive them."

Prayer

JESUS, dear Jesus, we all will soon be laid to rest, returning to dust. Let us then while we still have life not cling to the earth but soar to the heavens.

Help me to pray with untiring earnestness and give myself cheerfully to Your service. You said that first of all and most of all we should pray. Give me the grace to pray faithfully. Amen.

In accordance with the custom of those condemned to death, Jesus is scourged.

Day 27

Jesus, Victim for Our Sins

WHEN people turned from Jesus' message back to their drudgery and daily work, they could not forget what He said and they could not forget Him. They could not fathom Christ's wisdom but they knew it was beautiful, and His words stuck in their hearts. There was something unearthly about Him. They knew too that He cared for them. They admired Him. He faced the full impact of evil and in dying took on our burdens. He suffered the ridiculous trial, the buffeting and buffoonery, the mocking and scourging, and the torture on the Cross.

St. Athanasius said, "The Son of God was made the Son of Man that the children of man might be made children of God." St. Irenaeus said, "His hands are stretched out to gather all men together." St. Peter said, "This Jesus Whom you crucified, there is salvation in no other."

Jesus said, "You are My friends." I came that you should have life and have it to the full." "I am ready to die for you, I love you so much."

God stooping down gave us the Light to walk by. He sent His Son, mercy descended upon the earth, and the wilderness, a desolate land, brought forth blossoms of beauty and leaping joy.

The great work of Christ was drinking the cup, bowing to the Will of the Father. The face of Christ is a face of love and kindness. When we are kind, we have the face of Christ.

Prayer

HOW great is the name of God through all the land. How wonderful You are, O Jesus. You are holy and good. Preserve me, for I take refuge in You.

Lord, You are my portion. Show me the path to follow. Give me the courage to walk after You. I keep You ever in my sight and my soul is glad and I am at peace. Amen.

*On the Cross, Jesus offers His life to atone
for the sins of the world.*

Day 28

Jesus, Redeemer of the World

JESUS said He was the Good Shepherd and the Good Shepherd gives His life for His sheep. This He did. And the Good Shepherd goes out in search of the lost sheep and rejoices when He finds him and carries him home joyfully. The sinner is the lost sheep. We are all sinners.

He was a Person of forgiveness. Just before He gave up His Spirit, He said, "Father, forgive them."

They executed Christ on a hill amid great horror and the howling of the mob. But His sane, clear voice forgave the good thief, entrusted John to take care of His Mother, and gave Mary to us to be our Mother also. He was always thinking of others, even in agony on the Cross.

Jesus was the Savior Who dies for us to save our souls. On the Cross He said, "I thirst." He thirsted for souls. He always loves sinners and always wishes to help them.

In the crucifixion, evil and darkness triumphed, but only for a day. In the Resurrection, the strength of evil was turned to weakness and worldly wisdom became folly. But the worldly wise could not save the world, they only plunged it deeper into darkness. Jesus did save the world. When weakness and softness were dissolving society, Jesus with strength and courage redeemed us.

Prayer

DEAR Jesus, in dying on the Cross, Your love for us was supremely revealed. Please let Your love captivate our minds and stir our hearts. Let us be incorporated into You, our lives interwoven with You so that we can glorify God.

On Calvary was the great attack of evil on love. You endured all. You outdistance by far everyone in generosity and humility. Thank You, Jesus. Amen.

*An Angel announces to the women that
Jesus has risen from the dead.*

Day 29

Jesus, Our Life and Resurrection

OUR days come to an end like a sigh. They
are soon gone and we fly away," says the
Psalmist. Each day it is more necessary to
look to Christ.

Mary Magdalene said, "They have taken
away my Lord and I don't know where they
have laid Him." This is the lot of many people
today. Our society with endless distractions
takes Christ from us. We don't know where
He is in modern life. But we must find Him.
We will do so on our knees.

Jesus died a terrible death for us out of
pure love. With limitless love, He stretched

out His arms on the Cross to be nailed to the wood. He was born to redeem us. Good Friday was the day that changed the world forever. The Cross of death was the tree of life. Death now is dead.

Jesus triumphed on Easter. The crucified Christ rose from the tomb. As St. Paul exclaims, "O death, where is your victory? O death, where is your sting?"

Death is dreaded by the pagans, but for the Christian it is the door through which we pass from this life to the next life. And Jesus, our dearest Friend, is the first to greet us on the other side of the door of death. We cannot exile Him then to the edge of existence; He must be central.

We should turn to Christ, and be alive with the life of the Risen Christ.

Prayer

JESUS, I thank You with all my heart for Your goodness and Your help. You never waiver. You go on offering Yourself and Your gifts to me. No heart is more tender to sinners, the afflicted, and the needy.

I turn to You and beg You for Your assistance for me and my family and loved ones and all who are in need. Please especially bless those who die today. Amen.

The Risen Jesus ascends to His heavenly Father and is seated at His right hand in glory.

Day 30

Jesus, Seated in Glory

JESUS is not like anyone else. His words are from heaven. Only if we believe in Jesus do we dare to believe in man. In Him we understand ourselves and other people.

Jesus calls out to all. The Church exists to introduce us to Christ. In the Church we see Jesus. The face of Jesus is shown to us.

It is Jesus Who heals our suffering. From His seat at the Father's right hand to which He ascended after His Resurrection, He comforts us in our sorrows. He is our Savior. Jesus is the key to life, the opener of doors, the light in the darkness, our Shepherd, the guide on the right road for us. Christ is the image of God, and God is Love. We too must be loving, giving individuals. In our time men's interests have turned in upon themselves. This is not the way to be happy, even though TV and the media tell us it is—so they can sell their products.

Jesus came to heal the sick and the suffering and so had to become one of them. He was a self-emptying person. He is the pledge of God's love. Peevish hearts are confounded by the generosity of Jesus, but those who open their hearts to Him strive to be like Him.

God, the Incomprehensible, sent His Son in poverty, weakness, and suffering. He revived and restored our nature, making it newborn. Christ came to reclaim for God the world that had lain so long in darkness. He came to help us gain eternal life.

Prayer

JESUS, our nature at times resents confinement. We do not like rules. We do not like to obey the Ten Commandments. Help me, Lord.

God's rules were given us for our good and the good of society, but our contrary nature seeks to shake off the harness. In doing so, we hurt ourselves most of all. Help me, Jesus. Amen.

Jesus is King in a kingdom of truth and life, holiness and grace, and justice, love, and peace.

Day 31

Jesus, Our King

JESUS was a king, but more than a king; His was a spiritual kingdom. And He is one of the immortal men of history, One that people can never forget.

Jesus cannot be written about as other men. His words are too important for such an approach. He is a unique figure, a great personality, One Who instructs all in the ways of God, and in the way to God.

He was born humbly, lived in poverty in a little land, and was killed at an early age because He was too good for evil men to let live. But of His greatness, there is no doubt.

His remarkable life is the turning point in history. His words affect countless lives even in our own times.

What Jesus said is vital. He disclosed the character of God and showed the way people can live together in the world: we must have sympathy, understanding, and a kind spirit for one another.

Jesus, Son of God, cannot teach us falsely, for God is Truth. Pilate said to Christ, "What is truth?" and then would not wait for an answer. So many today are like that.

But those who listen to Jesus know the truth in our world, which is often a jungle of lies, deceit, and darkness. On Calvary, Truth was murdered between two thieves. Truth is silent. The thieves are crying out. Truth today is discovered in silent prayer amid all the noise in our society. Jesus is our Teacher. Let us pray. Let us listen to Him in silence.

Prayer

O JESUS, help me to take time for You, to listen to You, to pray to You. Without You, life is a jungle.

We are like a lost baby at night in the wilderness. We don't know which way to go, while those who try to destroy us are all around on every side. Help us, Jesus, guard us, guide us, bless us. Amen.

*The following prayers enable us to draw
near to Jesus and ask His help as the
Roman centurion did.*

PRAYERS TO JESUS

DAILY PRAYERS

Morning Offering

O JESUS, through the Immaculate Heart of
Mary, I offer You my prayers, works, joys
and sufferings of this day for all the intentions
of Your Sacred Heart, in union with the Holy
Sacrifice of the Mass throughout the world, in
reparation for my sins, for the intentions of all
our associates, and in particular for all the
intentions of this month (mention intention if
known).

Prayer for God's Protection and Christ's Presence

AS I arise today,
may the strength of God pilot me,
the power of God uphold me,
the wisdom of God guide me.

May the eye of God look before me,
the ear of God hear me,
the word of God speak for me.

May the hand of God protect me,
the way of God lie before me,
the shield of God defend me,
the host of God save me.

May Christ shield me today . . .
Christ with me, Christ before me,
Christ behind me,
Christ in me, Christ beneath me,
Christ above me,

Christ on my right, Christ on my left,
Christ when I lie down, Christ when I sit,
Christ when I stand,

Christ in the heart of everyone
who thinks of me,
Christ in the mouth of everyone
who speaks of me,

Christ in every eye that sees me,
Christ in every ear that hears me. Amen.

(St. Patrick)

Midafternoon Prayer

O DIVINE Savior, I transport myself in spirit to Mount Calvary to ask pardon for my sins, for it was because of humankind's sins that You chose to offer Yourself in sacrifice. I thank You for your extraordinary generosity and I am also grateful to You for making me a child of Mary, Your Mother.

Blessed Mother, take me under your protection. St. John, you took Mary under your care. Teach me true devotion to Mary, the Mother of God. May the Father, the Son, and the Holy Spirit be glorified in all places through the Immaculate Virgin Mary. Amen.

Petitions of St. Augustine

L ORD Jesus, let me know myself; let me know You,
And desire nothing else but You.
Let me hate myself and love You,
And do all things for the sake of You.
Let me humble myself and exalt You,
And think of nothing else but You.
Let me die to myself and live in You,
And take whatever happens as coming from
    You.
Let me forsake myself and walk after You,
And ever desire to follow You.
Let me flee from myself and turn to You,
That so I may merit to be defended by You.

Let me fear for myself, let me fear You,
And be among those that are chosen by You.
Let me distrust myself and trust in You,
And ever obey for the love of You.
Let me cleave to nothing but You,
And ever be poor because of You.
Look upon me that I may love You,
Call me, that I may see You,
And forever possess You, for all eternity.
  Amen.

Night Prayer

JESUS Christ, my God, I adore You and I thank You for the many favors You have bestowed on me this day. I offer You my sleep and all the moments of this night, and I pray You to preserve me from sin. Therefore, I place myself in Your most sacred Side, and under the mantle of our Blessed Lady, my Mother. May the holy Angels assist me and keep me in peace, and may Your blessing be upon me. Amen.

Prayer for the Faithful Departed

O LORD Jesus Christ, King of glory, deliver the souls of all the faithful departed from the pains of hell and from the bottomless pit; deliver them from the lion's mouth, that hell swallow them not up, that they fall not into darkness, but let the holy standard-bearer Michael bring them into that holy light which You promised to Abraham and his seed. Amen.

CONFESSION PRAYERS

Prayer before Confession

RECEIVE my confession, O most loving and gracious Lord Jesus Christ, only hope for the salvation of my soul. Grant to me true contrition of soul, so that day and night I may by penance make satisfaction for my many sins. Savior of the world, O good Jesus, Who gave Yourself to the death on the Cross to save sinners, look upon me, most wretched of all sinners; have pity on me, and give me the light to know my sins, true sorrow for them, and a purpose of never committing them again.

O gracious Virgin Mary, Immaculate Mother of Jesus, I implore you to obtain for me by your powerful intercession these graces from your Divine Son.

St. Joseph, pray for me. Amen.

Prayer after Confession

MY dearest Jesus, I have told all my sins as well as I could. I have tried hard to make a good confession. I feel sure that You have forgiven me. I thank You. It is only because of all Your sufferings that I can go to confession and free myself from my sins. Your Heart is full of love and mercy for poor sinners. I love You because You are so good to me.

My loving Savior, I shall try to keep from sin and to love You more each day. My dear Mother Mary, pray for me and help me to keep my promises. Protect me and do not let me fall back into sin. Amen.

PRAYERS BEFORE HOLY COMMUNION

Act of Faith

LORD Jesus Christ, I firmly believe that You are present in this Blessed Sacrament as true God and true Man, with Your Body and Blood, Soul and Divinity. My Redeemer and my Judge, I adore Your divine majesty in union with the Angels and Saints. I believe, O Lord; increase my faith. Amen.

Act of Hope

GOOD Jesus, in You alone I place all my hope. You are my salvation and my strength, the source of all good. Through Your mercy, through Your Passion and death, I hope to obtain the pardon of my sins, the grace of final perseverance, and a happy eternity. Amen.

Act of Love

JESUS, my God, I love You with my whole heart and above all things, because You are the one supreme Good and an infinitely perfect Being. You have given Your life for me, a poor sinner, and in Your mercy You have even offered Yourself as food for my soul. My God, I love You. Inflame my heart so that I may love You more. Amen.

Act of Contrition

O MY Savior, I am truly sorry for having offended You because You are infinitely good and sin displeases You. I detest all the sins of my life and I desire to atone for them. Through the merits of Your Precious Blood, wash me of all stain of sin, so that entirely cleansed I may worthily approach the most holy Sacrament of the altar. Amen.

PRAYERS AFTER
HOLY COMMUNION

Act of Faith

JESUS, I firmly believe that You are present within me as God and Man, to enrich my soul with graces and to fill my heart with the happiness of the blessed. I believe that You are Christ, the Son of the living God. Amen.

Act of Adoration

WITH deepest humility, I adore You, my Lord and my God; You have made my soul Your dwelling place. I adore You as my Creator from Whose hands I came and with Whom I am to be happy forever. Amen.

Act of Love

DEAR Jesus, I love You with my whole heart, with my whole soul, and with all my strength. May the love of Your own Sacred Heart fill my soul and purify it so that I may die to the world for love of You, as You died on the Cross for love of me.

My God, You are all mine; grant that I may be all Yours in time and in eternity. Amen.

Act of Thanksgiving

DEAR Lord, I thank You from the depths of my heart for Your infinite kindness in coming to me. With Your most holy Mother and all the Angels, I praise Your mercy and generosity toward me, a poor sinner. I thank You for nourishing my soul with Your Sacred Body and Precious Blood. I will try to show my gratitude to You in the Sacrament of Your love, by obedience to Your holy commandments, by fidelity to my duties, by kindness to my neighbor, and by an earnest endeavor to become more like You in my daily conduct. Amen.

Prayer to Our Redeemer

SOUL of Christ, sanctify me. Body of Christ, save me. Water from the side of Christ, wash me. Blood of Christ, inebriate me. Passion of Christ, strengthen me. O good Jesus, hear me. Within Thy wounds hide me. Suffer me not to be separated from Thee. From the malignant enemy, defend me. At the hour of death, call me, and bid me come to Thee, that with Thy saints I may praise Thee forever and ever. Amen.

Prayer to See Jesus in Others

THROUGH this Holy Communion, I beg You, O Lord Jesus, for the grace ever to love You in my neighbor. Let me see in every human being Your own dear Self—disguised but really there. Since every human being is a potential member of Your mystical Body, I want to make my every act a personal service rendered to You.

Your new law demands that I avoid not only bodily injury to my neighbor but also angry and uncharitable words and emotions. Let me never put limits to my forgiveness, so that Your Father may forgive me my offenses. Through this Communion make me a living example of Your great commandment of love. Amen.

Prayer to Christ the King, p. 94.

PRAYERS TO JESUS IN THE BLESSED SACRAMENT

Prayer of Adoration and Petition

I ADORE You, O Jesus, true God and true Man, here present in the Holy Eucharist, as I humbly kneel before You and unite myself in spirit with all the faithful on earth and all the Saints in heaven.

In heartfelt gratitude for so great a blessing, I love You, my Jesus, with my whole soul, for You are infinitely perfect and all worthy of my love. Give me the grace never more in any way to offend You. Grant that I may be renewed by Your Eucharistic presence here on earth and be found worthy to arrive with Mary at the enjoyment of Your eternal and blessed presence in heaven. Amen.

Prayer of Reparation

WITH that deep and humble feeling which the Faith inspires in me, O my God and Savior, Jesus Christ, true God and true Man, I love You with all my heart, and I adore You Who are hidden here. I do so in reparation for all the irreverences, profanations, and sacrileges which You receive in the most august Sacrament of the Altar.

I adore You, O my God, but not so much as You are worthy to be adored. Please accept my good will and help me in my weakness.

Would that I could adore You with that perfect worship which the Angels in heaven are able to offer You. O Jesus, may You be adored, loved, and thanked by all people at every moment in this most holy Sacrament. Amen.

Act of Spiritual Communion

MY JESUS, I believe that You are truly present in the most Blessed Sacrament. I love You above all things and I desire to possess You within my soul. Since I am unable now to receive You sacramentally, come at least spiritually into my heart. I embrace You as being already there and unite myself entirely to You. Never permit me to be separated from You. Amen.

O Sacred Banquet

O SACRED Banquet, in which Christ is received, the memory of His Passion is renewed, the mind is filled with grace, and a pledge of future glory is given to us.

℣. You have given them bread from heaven.

℟. Containing in itself all sweetness.

Let us pray:

O GOD, since You have left us a remembrance of Your Passion beneath the veils of this Sacrament, grant us, we pray, so to venerate the sacred mysteries of Your Body and Blood that we may always enjoy the fruits of Your Redemption. Who live and reign forever. Amen.

Hidden God, Devoutly I Adore You
(Adoro Te Devote)

HIDDEN God, devoutly I adore You,
Truly present underneath these veils:
All my heart subdues itself before You
Since it all before You faints and fails.

Not to sight, or taste, or touch be credit,
Hearing only do we trust secure;
I believe, for God the Son has said it—
Word of Truth that ever shall endure.

On the Cross was veiled Your Godhead's
  splendor,
Here Your manhood lies hidden too;
Unto both alike my faith I render,
And, as sued the contrite thief, I sue.

Though I look not on Your wounds with
  Thomas,
You, my Lord, and You, my God, I call:
Make me more and more believe Your prom-
  ise,
Hope in You, and love You over all.

O memorial of my Savior dying,
Living Bread, that gives life to man;

Make my soul, its life from You supplying,
Taste Your sweetness, as on earth it can.

Deign, O Jesus, Pelican of heaven,
Me, a sinner, in Your Blood to lave,
To a single drop of which is given
All the world from all its sin to save.

Contemplating, Lord, Your hidden presence,
Grant me what I thirst for and implore,
In the revelation of Your essence
To behold Your glory evermore. Amen.

PRAYERS TO THE CHILD JESUS

Adoration

JESUS, Son of the glorious Virgin Mary and
only Son of the living God, I adore You and
acknowledge You as my God, the only true
God, one and infinitely perfect.

You have made out of nothing all things
that are outside of You, and You preserve and
govern them with infinite wisdom, sovereign
goodness, and supreme power.

I beg of You, by the mysteries that were fulfilled in Your sacred Humanity, to cleanse me
in Your Blood from all my past sins. Pour
forth abundantly upon me Your Holy Spirit,
together with His grace, His virtues, and His
gifts.

Make me believe in You, hope in You, love
You, and labor to merit the possession of You

through each of my actions. Give Yourself to me some day in the brightness of Your glory, in the company of all Your Saints. Amen.

Prayer to the Infant Jesus of Prague

DEAR Jesus, Little Infant of Prague, how tenderly You love us. Your greatest joy is to dwell among us and to bestow Your blessing upon us. So many who turned to You with confidence have received graces and had their petitions granted. I also come before You now with this special request (mention it).

Dear Infant, rule over me and do with me and mine as You will, for I know that in Your divine wisdom and love You will arrange everything for the best. Do not withdraw Your hand from me, but protect and bless me forever.

Dear Infant, help me in my needs. Make me truly happy with You in time and in eternity, and I shall thank You forever with all my heart. Amen.

PRAYERS TO THE HOLY NAME OF JESUS

Prayer of Praise

O GLORIOUS Name of Jesus, gracious Name, Name of love and of power! Through You sins are forgiven, enemies are vanquished, the sick are freed from illness, the suffering are made strong and cheerful. You bring honor to those who believe, instruction to those who preach, strength to those who toil, and sustenance to those who are weary.

Our love for You is ardent and glowing, our prayers are heard, the souls of those who contemplate You are filled to overflowing, and all the blessed in heaven are filled with Your glory. Grant that we too may reign with them through this Your most Holy Name. Amen.

Prayer for Divine Love

O LORD Jesus Christ, Who said, "Ask, and it shall be given you; seek, and you shall find; knock, and it shall be opened to you," mercifully hear our prayers, and grant us the gift of Your most Divine Love, that we may ever love You with our whole hearts, and in all our words and actions, and never cease from Your praise.

Give us, O Lord, a perpetual fear and love of Your Holy Name; for You never cease to govern those whom You instruct in the solidity of Your love. Who live and reign world without end. Amen.

PRAYERS TO THE SACRED HEART OF JESUS

Prayer of Consecration

I, N . . . , give myself to the Sacred Heart of our Lord Jesus Christ, and I consecrate to Him my person and my life, my actions, pains, and sufferings, so that henceforth I shall be unwilling to make use of any part of my being except for the honor, love, and glory of the Sacred Heart. My unchanging purpose is to be all His and to do all things for the love of Him while renouncing with all my heart whatever is displeasing to Him.

I take You, O Sacred Heart, as the only object of my love, the guardian of my life, the assurance of my salvation, the remedy of my weakness and inconstancy, the atonement for all my faults, and the sure refuge at my death.

O Heart of goodness, be my justification before God the Father, and turn away from me the strokes of His righteous anger.

O Heart of love, I place all my trust in You, for I fear everything from my own wickedness and frailty, but I hope for all things from Your goodness and bounty.

Consume in me all that can displease You or resist Your holy Will. Let Your pure love imprint You so deeply upon my heart that I shall nevermore be able to forget You or be separated from You. May I obtain from all Your loving kindness the grace of having my name written in You, for I desire to place in You all my happiness and all my glory, living and dying in virtual bondage to You. Amen.

(St. Margaret Mary Alacoque)

Memorare

REMEMBER, most sweet Jesus, that no one was ever abandoned who had recourse to Your Sacred Heart, implored Its help, or called for mercy. Filled with this confidence, Divine Heart, ruler of all hearts, I come to You, oppressed beneath the weight of my sins.

Do not reject my poor prayers, but listen to them mercifully, and be pleased to answer them. You have the Heart of the best of fathers. May God, Who has deigned to give You to us for our salvation, receive my prayers through You. Amen.

Prayer for Enlightenment

SACRED Heart of Jesus, teach me an entire forgetfulness of myself, since there is no other way of reaching You. Grant that I may do nothing that is not worthy of You.

Teach me what I ought to do to attain to Your pure love, for You have inspired me with this desire. I feel in myself a great longing to please You. But I am helpless without Your special light and strength.

O Lord, do Your Will in me, though I often opposed it in the past. You must do all, divine Heart of Jesus. It shall be Your glory alone if I become a Saint, and it is for Your glory alone that I desire to be perfect. Amen.

(St. Claude de la Colombiere)

Litany of the Most Sacred Heart of Jesus

LORD, have mercy.
Christ, have mercy.
Lord, have mercy.
Christ, hear us.
Christ, graciously hear us.
God the Father of heaven, *have mercy on us.**
God the Son, Redeemer of the world,
God, the Holy Spirit,
Holy Trinity, one God,
Heart of Jesus, Son of the Eternal Father,
Heart of Jesus, formed by the Holy Spirit in the womb of the Virgin Mother,
Heart of Jesus, substantially united to the Word of God,
Heart of Jesus, of infinite majesty,

Heart of Jesus, sacred temple of God,
Heart of Jesus, tabernacle of the Most High,
Heart of Jesus, house of God and gate of heaven,
Heart of Jesus, burning furnace of charity,
Heart of Jesus, abode of justice and love,
Heart of Jesus, full of goodness and love,
Heart of Jesus, abyss of all virtues,
Heart of Jesus, most worthy of all praise,
Heart of Jesus, king and center of all hearts,
Heart of Jesus, in Whom are all the treasures of wisdom

* *Have mercy on us* is repeated after each invocation.

and knowledge,

Heart of Jesus, in Whom dwells the fullness of Divinity,

Heart of Jesus, in Whom the Father was well pleased,

Heart of Jesus, of Whose fullness we have all received,

Heart of Jesus, desire of the everlasting hills,

Heart of Jesus, patient and most merciful,

Heart of Jesus, enriching all who invoke You,

Heart of Jesus, fountain of life and holiness,

Heart of Jesus, propitiation for our sins,

Heart of Jesus, loaded down with opprobrium,

Heart of Jesus, bruised for our offenses,

Heart of Jesus, obedient to death,

Heart of Jesus, pierced with a lance,

Heart of Jesus, source of all consolation,

Heart of Jesus, our life and resurrection,

Heart of Jesus, our peace and reconciliation,

Heart of Jesus, victim for our sins,

Heart of Jesus, salvation of those who trust in You,

Heart of Jesus, hope of those who die in You,

Heart of Jesus, delight of all the Saints,

Lamb of God, You take away the sins of the world; *spare us, O Lord.*

Lamb of God, You take away the sins of the world; *graciously hear us, O Lord.*

Lamb of God, You take away the sins of the world; *have mercy on us.*

℣. Jesus, meek and humble of heart.

℟. *Make our hearts like to Yours.*

L ET us pray.
Almighty and Eternal God,
look upon the Heart of Your most beloved Son
and upon the praises and satisfaction
which He offers You in the name of sinners;
and to those who implore Your mercy,
in Your great goodness, grant forgiveness
in the Name of the same Jesus Christ, Your Son,
Who lives and reigns with You, forever and ever.
℞. Amen.

PRAYERS TO THE PRECIOUS BLOOD OF JESUS

Act of Reparation

P RECIOUS Blood of Jesus, infinite price of sinful man's redemption, both drink and laver of our souls! You continually plead the cause of man before the throne of infinite mercy. From the depths of my heart I adore You. Jesus, so far as I am able, I want to make reparation for the insults and outrages You constantly receive from human beings, especially from those who dare to blaspheme You.

Who would not venerate this Blood of infinite value? Who does not feel inflamed with love for Jesus, Who shed It? What would become of me had I not been redeemed by this divine Blood? Who has drained It all from the veins of my Savior? Surely, this was the work of love!

O infinite love, which has given us this saving balm! O balm beyond all price, welling up from the fountain of infinite love! Grant that every heart and every tongue may praise and thank You now and forever. Amen.

Petitions in Honor of the Precious Blood

PRECIOUS Blood of Jesus, shed in the circumcision, make me pure of mind, heart, and body.

Precious Blood, oozing from every pore of Jesus in the Agony, enable me to love God's holy Will above all.

Precious Blood, flowing abundantly in the scourging at the pillar, inspire me with a keen sorrow for my sins, and a high-level tolerance of suffering.

Precious Blood, falling in profusion from the crown of thorns, grant me a ready acceptance of humiliations.

Precious Blood, shed so profusely in the crucifixion of our Lord, make me die entirely to self-love.

Precious Blood, shed to the very last drop by the opening of Christ's Sacred Heart, give me that generous love which sacrifices all for God.

Precious Blood, sacred price of my redemption, apply to me Your infinite merits.

Precious Blood of Jesus, I adore You from the depths of my heart; I invoke You ardently for You are my salvation, and by You I hope to obtain the joys of heaven. Amen.

PRAYERS TO JESUS CRUCIFIED

Prayer to Jesus on the Cross

O JESUS, for how many ages have You been on the Cross and yet people pass by in utter disregard of You except to pierce once again Your Sacred Heart. How often have I myself passed You by, heedless of Your overwhelming sorrow, Your countless wounds, and Your infinite love! How often have I myself stood before You, not to comfort and console You, but to offend You by my conduct or neglect You, and to scorn Your love!

You have stretched out Your hands to comfort me, and I have seized those hands—that might have consigned me to hell—and have bent them back upon the Cross, nailing them rigid and helpless to it. Yet I have only succeeded in imprinting my name on Your palms forever. You have loved me with an infinite love and I have taken advantage of that love to sin all the more against You.

Yet my ingratitude has only succeeded in piercing Your Sacred Heart and causing Your Precious Blood to flow forth upon me. O Jesus, let Your Blood be upon me not for a curse but for a blessing. Lamb of God, You take away the sins of the world; have mercy on me. Amen.

Look Down Upon Me, Good and Gentle Jesus

LOOK down upon me, good and gentle Jesus, while before Your face I humbly kneel, and with burning soul pray and beseech You to fix deep in my heart lively sentiments of faith, hope and charity, true contrition for my sins, and a firm purpose of amendment, while I contemplate with great love and tender pity Your five wounds, pondering over them within me, calling to mind the words which David, Your prophet, said of You, my good Jesus: "They have pierced My hands and My feet; they have numbered all My bones." Amen.   *(Psalm 22:17-18)*

PRAYERS TO CHRIST THE KING

Act of Dedication of the Human Race to Jesus Christ King

MOST sweet Jesus, Redeemer of the human race, look down upon us humbly prostrate before You. We are Yours, and Yours we wish to be; but to be more surely united with You, behold, each one of us freely consecrates himself today to Your Most Sacred Heart. Many indeed have never known You; many, too, despising Your precepts, have rejected You. Have mercy on them all, most merciful Jesus, and draw them to Your Sacred Heart.

Be King, O Lord, not only of the faithful who have never forsaken You, but also of the prodigal children who have abandoned You; grant that they may quickly return to their Father's house, lest they die of wretchedness and hunger.

Be King of those who are deceived by erroneous opinions, or whom discord keeps aloof, and call them back to the harbor of truth and the unity of faith, so that soon there may be but one flock and one Shepherd.

Grant, O Lord, to Your Church assurance of freedom and immunity from harm; give tranquility of order to all nations; make the earth resound from pole to pole with one cry: Praise to the divine Heart that wrought our salvation; to It be glory and honor for ever. Amen.

Act of Consecration

O CHRIST JESUS, I acknowledge You as King of the universe. All that has been made has been created for You. Make full use of Your rights over me. I renew the promises I made in Baptism, when I renounced Satan and all his pomps and works. I promise to live a good Christian life. Especially, I undertake to help, to the extent of my means, to secure the triumph of the rights of God and of Your Church.

Divine Heart of Jesus, I offer You my poor efforts so that all hearts may acknowledge Your sacred Royalty, and the kingdom of Your peace may be established throughout the entire universe. Amen.